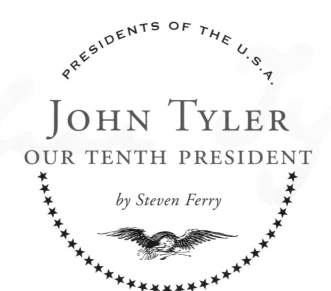

PRESIDENTS OF THE U.S.A.

John Tyler
OUR TENTH PRESIDENT

by Steven Ferry

THE CHILD'S WORLD ®

Published in the United States of America

The Child's World®
1980 Lookout Drive • Mankato, MN 56003-1705
800-599-READ • www.childsworld.com

Acknowledgments
The Child's World®: Mary Berendes, Publishing Director

Creative Spark: Mary McGavic, Project Director; Melissa McDaniel, Editorial
Director; Deborah Goodsite, Photo Research

The Design Lab: Kathleen Petelinsek, Design; Gregory Lindholm, Page Production

Content Adviser: David R. Smith, Adjunct Assistant Professor of History,
University of Michigan–Ann Arbor

Photos
Cover and page 3: White House Historical Association (White House Collection),
(detail); White House Historical Association (White House Collection)

Interior: The Art Archive: 4 (Culver Pictures); Art Resource, NY: 9 and 38 (The
Newark Museum), 28 (National Portrait Gallery, Smithsonian Institution);
Associated Press Images: 13; Benjamin Harrison Presidential Site: 19; The
Bridgeman Art Library: 17 (Collection of the New-York Historical Society); Corbis:
20, 29 (Corbis), 33 (Dave G. Houser), 37 (Richard T. Nowitz); The Granger
Collection, New York: 10, 14 and 38, 15, 16, 18 and 39, 21, 22, 26, 27; The
Image Works: 5 (Mary Evans Picture Library); iStockphoto: 44 (Tim Fan); Library
of Congress: 12, 24, 31; North Wind Picture Archives: 35 (North Wind); Picture
History: 30, 32, 34 and 39; Sherwood Forest Plantation, Charles City, VA: 7, 8,
25; College of William and Mary: 6 (University Archives Photograph Collection,
Special Collections Research Center, Swem Library); SuperStock: 11 (SuperStock,
Inc.); U.S. Air Force photo: 45; White House Historical Association (White House
Collection), (detail): 36.

Library of Congress Cataloging–in–Publication Data
Ferry, Steven, 1953–
  John Tyler / by Steven Ferry.
      p. cm. — (Presidents of the U.S.A.)
  Includes bibliographical references and index.
  ISBN 978–1–60253–039–3 (library bound : alk. paper)
  1. Tyler, John, 1790–1862—Juvenile literature. 2. Presidents—United States—
Biography—Juvenile literature. I. Title.

E397.F46 2008
973.5'8092—dc22
  [B]
                                                    2007049062

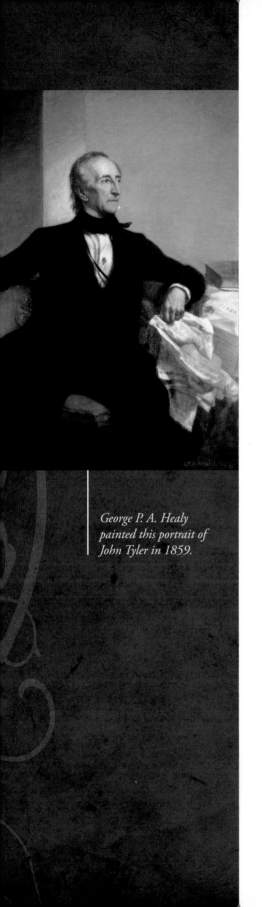

George P. A. Healy painted this portrait of John Tyler in 1859.

TABLE OF CONTENTS

A REBEL

John Tyler came from a family with deep roots in **politics** in England and America. He often said he was a distant relative of Wat Tyler, the leader of a peasant revolt against Richard II of England. When the king wanted to increase taxes, Wat and his followers led a rebellion, a battle against the English government. But Wat was soon killed, and his rebellion was crushed. Like Wat, who was brave enough to stand up to King Richard II, John Tyler was also a brave man. He often stood up for what he believed. Just like Wat, he often lost.

Henry Tyler, John's great-grandfather, came to America from England in 1653. He settled near Williamsburg, Virginia. The family enjoyed success in their new homeland. By the time future president John Tyler was born on March 29, 1790, the Tyler family owned a large tobacco farm, called a plantation,

John Tyler became president in 1841.

which was named Greenway. It was on the James River between Richmond and Williamsburg. The Tylers also owned 40 slaves, who worked hard to run the plantation. John's mother, Mary, died in 1797. After this sad event, his father, Judge John Tyler, lovingly raised John and his seven brothers and sisters.

Judge Tyler was a school friend and admirer of the third American president, Thomas Jefferson. Like

Wat Tyler, the leader of a peasant revolt, is killed while King Richard II looks on.

The home where John Tyler was born is still standing. It is privately owned and closed to the public.

John Tyler attended the College of William and Mary. Founded in 1693, it is the second-oldest college in the United States.

Jefferson, Judge Tyler was an independent man who supported the American Revolution, the war in which the United States won its freedom from Great Britain. Tyler raised his children to believe firmly in the ideas of the U.S. **Constitution.** He told them exciting tales about the Revolution and the brave patriots who fought for liberty. Tyler was proud to be an American.

Although his son John was a gentle person, he led his own rebellion while he was still quite young. His schoolteacher was a strict, unkind man named William McMurdo. He often whipped students who misbe-haved, or even those who gave an incorrect answer. John grew tired of McMurdo's severe punishments. One day, he and the other schoolchildren knocked McMurdo to the floor, tied him up, and locked the school door behind them as they left. McMurdo lay on the floor all afternoon before a passerby freed him.

John Tyler grew up at Greenway, the Tyler family plantation in southeastern Virginia.

Judge Tyler did not punish his son for doing this. He was proud that John had rebelled against a tyrant, a person who uses his power unfairly.

In 1802, John enrolled in classes at the College of William and Mary in Williamsburg. He studied Latin, Greek, English literature, history, and mathematics before graduating in 1807 at age 17. He returned home determined to become a lawyer. He also dreamed of a career in politics. At the time, young men who wanted to study law did not go to law school. Instead, they worked with a lawyer as an apprentice to learn the profession. John studied law with his father and then with his cousin, Samuel Tyler.

One year earlier, John had met Letitia Christian. She was the shy and loving daughter of a wealthy Virginia merchant. John courted Letitia for five years,

John Tyler lived at Greenway in his youth. He later bought another Virginia plantation called Walnut Grove, which he renamed Sherwood Forest. His family has owned the estate ever since. In fact, Tyler's grandson still lives at the plantation today.

Tyler's father, Judge John Tyler, was college roommates with future president Thomas Jefferson. The elder Tyler served as governor of Virginia from 1808 to 1811.

Tyler was the first president born after the United States Constitution was adopted.

writing poems and playing the violin for her. He finally kissed her just a few weeks before they married in 1813, on his 23rd birthday. The couple would have eight children in the next 17 years, one of whom died at birth.

John Tyler passed his law exams in 1809. The opportunity to begin a career in politics came that same year. Judge Tyler had been elected governor of Virginia the year before, and John went to live with him in the state capital, Richmond. He began working at the law office of Edmund Randolph, who was the first U.S. attorney general while George Washington was president. An attorney general is a lawyer who handles a government's legal affairs.

With Randolph's help, Tyler became involved in politics. By 1811, he was elected to the Virginia state **legislature.** A long career in politics had begun.

THE VIRGINIA GENTRY

A small group of families controlled Virginia from colonial times through the Civil War. Many of these families traced their roots back to Virginia's earliest days. They had established large plantations during colonial times, and the toil of their slaves made them rich. By the mid-1700s, Virginia was the wealthiest of the American colonies.

The members of the Virginia **gentry** led elite, cultured lives. They built huge mansions, which they filled with the finest furniture from Europe. They read widely, establishing large libraries in their homes. Their children were well educated, often by private tutors. Children learned to ride horses, dance, and play music. Virginia's elite dressed in elegant clothes made of silk and fine wool. They sometimes held fancy balls, grand parties filled with music and dancing.

The Virginia gentry dominated the political life of the early United States. Six of the first ten presidents were from Virginia. George Washington was the first. John Tyler was the nation's tenth president. He was the last member of the Virginia gentry to become president.

CHAPTER TWO

FIGHTING FOR THE CONSTITUTION

Tyler was active during his first five years in the Virginia House of Delegates, which was one part of the state's legislature. He tried to make sure that his fellow lawmakers followed the **principles** of the U.S. Constitution. In many ways, the men who wrote the

Letitia Christian and John Tyler were engaged for five years before they married. Tyler often wrote her love letters. "To ensure your happiness is now my only object," he once wrote. "And whether I float or sink in the stream of fortune, you may be assured of this, that I will never cease to love you"

Tyler had a long career in politics. He served in the Virginia legislature, in Congress, and as governor of Virginia before becoming president.

Constitution wanted to limit the power of the **federal** government. They wanted to give people in the individual states the right to make decisions for themselves. Like many southerners, Tyler believed that strengthening the federal government would threaten states' rights. Southerners were especially worried that a strong national government would try to outlaw slavery.

Tyler fought federal control of the states in many ways. For example, he was against the Second Bank of the United States. This bank was in charge of the federal government's money. Tyler believed smaller banks in each state should have more control. The U.S. government also had begun giving public land to homesteaders, people who moved to the **frontier** to build homes and farms. Tyler believed the states should

When Tyler was elected to Congress, his wife did not join him in Washington. She preferred to stay in Virginia, caring for their large household and many children.

11

decide how to use their own land. He also was against the federal government giving money to the states. Instead, he believed each state should take care of itself, without accepting federal funds.

In 1816, Tyler was elected to represent Virginia in the U.S. House of Representatives, which is part of Congress. As a national lawmaker, he continued his battle to uphold the Constitution.

Tyler's family background helped him get to know many important people in Washington. He was soon a regular figure at the fancy parties thrown by Dolley Madison, the wife of President James Madison.

In 1818, General Andrew Jackson invaded eastern Florida, which was then controlled by the Spanish. The U.S. government had given Jackson permission to

After attacking the Seminoles in Georgia, Andrew Jackson and his troops crossed into Florida and seized Spanish land.

Dolley Madison was at the center of the Washington social scene. She was considered the perfect hostess— warm, fashionable, and gracious.

fight the Seminole Indians in Georgia, who had been attacking white settlers. But Jackson entered Florida as well. Once there, he and his troops attacked and killed many British and Spanish citizens in the region. They seized control of Florida.

Tyler felt Jackson had done something wrong. He had received no orders from the U.S. government to attack eastern Florida. The Constitution says that no single person, not even a general or a president, has the right to make such a serious decision. Yet Jackson had become an American hero because he had gained more land for the nation. Tyler spoke out against Jackson. He bravely ignored Jackson's popularity and stood up for what he believed. As always, Tyler felt it was more important to uphold the Constitution than to go along with popular opinions.

Europeans started the slave trade 300 years before John Tyler was born. By the time this practice was finally stopped, 10 million Africans had been kidnapped and forced into slavery in the Americas. Most slaves in the United States worked on southern cotton or tobacco plantations.

In 1820, Congress had to decide whether to allow slavery in new **territories** such as Missouri. Northerners were against expanding slavery. But southerners were concerned that if slavery were outlawed in new territories, the federal government might try to make it illegal in the South as well. Congress tried to give both sides part of what they wanted. The Missouri **Compromise** outlawed slavery in all U.S. lands north of a specific point. Tyler voted against the compromise because it limited the places where slavery was legal. He believed that the Constitution gave individual states the right to decide whether to allow it. Most other congressmen disagreed with Tyler, and they passed the Missouri Compromise.

During his time in Congress, Tyler more often than not voted for the losing side. His lack of success discouraged him. Tyler also suffered from poor health. He caught colds easily and had stomach problems. In 1821, he left Congress, returning home to Virginia.

But Tyler was not out of politics for long. Two years later, he was again elected to the Virginia House of Delegates. He served from 1823 to 1825. During the presidential election of 1824, Tyler supported John Quincy Adams,

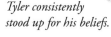

Tyler consistently stood up for his beliefs.

who was running against Andrew Jackson. Adams won the election. But soon after he took office, Tyler realized that the new president wanted to increase the federal government's power. Tyler was disappointed and refused to continue helping him.

In 1825, Tyler was elected governor of Virginia. He spent the next two years trying unsuccessfully to improve education and transportation in the state. Tyler grew frustrated with the job and again turned his attention to Washington. At the end of 1826, he was elected to the U.S. Senate.

Overseers look on as enslaved workers pick cotton. Like most southerners, John Tyler believed that each state had the right to decide for itself whether to allow slavery.

The Second Bank of the United States was often depicted as a monster. Here, President Andrew Jackson (left) is shown destroying the monster bank.

Tyler headed for the capital the following January and immediately joined the Democratic Party, which was preparing for the next election. The Democratic Party opposed John Quincy Adams and supported Andrew Jackson. Although Tyler did not fully believe in Jackson's ideas, he felt Jackson was a better choice for president than Adams. For one thing, Jackson, like Tyler, was against the Second Bank of the United States. Many Americans admired Jackson, and he easily won the presidential election of 1828.

Tyler soon came to disagree with President Jackson's plans for the nation. In 1833, Jackson signed the Force **Bill.** This gave the president the power to send federal troops into a state if it refused to obey laws. Tyler believed the bill was **unconstitutional,** but he was the only senator to oppose it. When Jackson removed all U.S. government funds from the Second Bank of the United States, Tyler decided not to support Jackson anymore. Tyler may have disliked the bank, but Jackson had acted without the necessary approval from Congress. The Constitution says that the president cannot make such a decision unless Congress agrees to it.

Throughout his career, Tyler was committed to states' rights. He believed the federal government's powers should be limited to those described in the Constitution.

In 1838, Letitia Tyler suffered a stroke, which is a serious injury to the brain. It left her unable to walk, and she seldom left her bedroom after that.

Although Andrew Jackson (left) and John Tyler were both southern Democrats, they disagreed on many issues. When Tyler felt that Jackson had become too powerful, he left the Democratic Party.

Tyler and other senators decided that Jackson had to be punished. They voted to censure him. When Congress censures the president, its members state formally that they think he has done something wrong. Jackson replied to the censure by saying he did not have to do what the Senate wanted. In 1836, leaders from Virginia ordered their senators to cancel the censure. Tyler refused to do so. He left his position instead. As always, he refused to do something he felt was wrong.

By this time, Tyler had left the Democratic Party and joined a new **political party,** the Whigs. The Whig Party was formed to oppose President Jackson and his policies.

People in Virginia still believed Tyler was a good leader. Two years later, he was reelected to the Virginia

Andrew Jackson leads Martin Van Buren over a pile of log cabins, symbols of William Henry Harrison's presidential campaign. Harrison defeated Van Buren in the 1840 presidential election.

Our cause our country, Our champion general.

W^M H. HARRISON, OUR BRAVE DEFENDER.

J. PIERSON.

General William Henry Harrison gained fame for leading U.S. troops in battle against Native Americans. This poster touts him as the nation's "brave defender."

House of Delegates. The other lawmakers elected him Speaker of the House in 1839. This meant he took charge of all their meetings.

In 1840, it was time for another election. The Whig Party needed to choose a presidential **candidate,** and they nominated a former war hero from the North named William Henry Harrison. The party chose Tyler to run as vice president, in part because he opposed Jackson. They also knew that many southerners would support Tyler. After all, he was from Virginia and owned slaves. Tyler did not agree with many of the Whigs' ideas, but the party believed he would not create problems as vice president. In December 1840, William Henry Harrison won the election, and Tyler became vice president.

William Henry Harrison ran for president for the first time in 1836. He lost the election of 1836 to Martin Van Buren, who had been Andrew Jackson's vice president. The Whig Party was disappointed when Van Buren won because he would keep Jackson's policies. They began campaigning for the next election right away. The 1840 election was a rematch between Harrison and Van Buren. This time, Harrison won.

19

ELECTIONS FOR THE PEOPLE

During the election of 1840, the Whig Party ran what was known as the "Hard Cider and Log Cabin Campaign." It changed the way elections were run in the United States. In earlier years, candidates had suggested what they thought were the most sensible solutions to the problems the nation faced. This allowed people to make intelligent decisions about how to vote. In 1840, the Whigs decided the best way to win the election was to entertain people and to insult the other candidate.

After the Whigs asked William Henry Harrison to run for president, they worked to create a positive image for him. They praised him as a war hero. To make him seem like a regular person, they said he lived on the frontier in a log cabin. In fact, he was actually from a wealthy family and he lived in a riverside mansion. The Whigs said Harrison liked to drink hard cider, which is an alcoholic drink made from apples, instead of expensive wines from foreign countries. They described his opponent, Martin Van Buren, as someone who lived like a king. They said Van Buren didn't understand the needs of the average American. They hoped this would increase Harrison's appeal to ordinary Americans.

During the campaign, Harrison traveled around the country in a wagon. It had a log cabin built on top of it. The wagon also carried a huge barrel of cider. At campaign stops, bands played music while people cheered. The Whigs passed out hard cider for everyone to drink. People chanted slogans such as "Van, Van, is a used-up man!" and "Tippecanoe and Tyler, too!" Tippecanoe was Harrison's nickname. He had been given it after leading U.S. Army troops to victory over the Shawnee Indians at the Battle of Tippecanoe in 1811.

AN ACCIDENTAL PRESIDENCY

Tyler's wife, Letitia, was quite ill when he became vice president. It would have been difficult for her to move to Washington. So Tyler planned to handle his duties from home, as vice presidents had done in the past. He traveled to the nation's capital to attend President Harrison's **inauguration.** The 68-year-old president had ridden on horseback to the Capitol. Then he gave the longest inaugural speech in history. He spoke for more than two hours in the freezing rain. He wore no hat or coat. That evening, Harrison came down with a cold.

John Tyler, 1841

The next day, Tyler returned to Virginia. Very soon, President Harrison's cold turned into a serious illness called **pneumonia.** Less than one

*William Henry
Harrison died at
the White House on
April 4, 1841. His
one-month presidency
was the shortest in
American history.*

month after his inauguration, Harrison lay sick in bed. Tyler had no idea the president was ill. Harrison died on April 4, 1841, but Tyler did not receive word until the next day.

No president had ever died in office before. The Constitution says that if the president dies, the vice president takes over the duties of the president. But the Constitution doesn't say the vice president actually becomes the president. Americans wondered what would happen next.

Tyler arrived in Washington on April 6. He met Harrison's **cabinet** members, who told him he was only the acting president. This meant he did not have the same powers a president would normally have. They would have to approve all his actions. "I am very glad to have in my cabinet such able **statesmen** as you," Tyler said. "But I can never consent to being dictated to as to what I shall or shall not do." Tyler stated firmly, "I am the president." He then said if any cabinet member opposed his decisions, he would be asked to give up his position.

Congress agreed with Tyler. It confirmed his presidency on April 9, 1841. But this did not stop many politicians from addressing letters to Tyler as "Acting President" and "Ex–Vice President." Tyler returned all these letters unopened.

Today, Americans know there is always a chance the president will die in office. They count on the government to keep working if this happens. Tyler's actions created the tradition that has since been followed when a U.S. president dies. At the time, however, Tyler's actions were controversial. Newspaper reporters and congressmen began calling him "His Accidency" or "the Accidental President." The cabinet refused to support him. Its members had expected to have a great deal of power, but Tyler would not allow this.

The new president had no advisers and no supporters in the government. And soon, he would have no political party. It became clear that Tyler would face many problems when the Whigs in Congress wanted to create another national bank. They passed two bills establishing a national bank. Tyler **vetoed** both of them. The fight over the national bank was just the first of many battles he would have with Congress.

These days, if a U.S. president dies, the vice president is automatically sworn into office and takes over the presidency. But when William Henry Harrison died, no one was sure what to do. John Tyler is credited with establishing the tradition of passing leadership on to the vice president.

Since Harrison's death, seven more presidents have died in office: Taylor, Lincoln, Garfield, McKinley, Harding, Roosevelt, and Kennedy.

President Tyler did not have a vice president.

In an effort to force Tyler out of office, all but one member of the cabinet resigned in the fall of 1841. Tyler replaced them within two days, selecting Democrats for the posts. The Whigs were furious and forced him out of the party. At the same time, Democrats did not trust Tyler because he had left their party years before. Most of the cabinet members did not keep their positions very long. During the rest of his presidential term, 22 men filled the six positions in his cabinet.

Without a stable cabinet or support from either party in Congress, Tyler could accomplish few of his goals. Tyler was the first president to face the possibility of **impeachment.** The Whigs in Congress tried to impeach him when he vetoed a **tariff** bill in 1842. They grew even angrier when he refused to replace all Democrats in government positions with people from

John Tyler receives news of President William Henry Harrison's death. Tyler was at his home in southern Virginia and did not even know that Harrison had been sick.

Tyler married Julia Gardiner in 1844. He was the first president to marry while in office.

the Whig Party. But Tyler believed in making decisions according to what was best for the nation, not what was best for a political party.

During this difficult time, Tyler also faced problems in his personal life. Letitia was confined to a wheelchair. She lived in an upstairs room at the White House. She came downstairs only once, to attend the wedding of their daughter Elizabeth. Letitia died just 17 months after Tyler entered office. Their daughter-in-law Priscilla Cooper Tyler acted as the White House hostess until 1844. That year, Tyler married a young woman from New York named Julia Gardiner.

Throughout his presidency, Tyler continued to veto bills with which he did not agree. He opposed bills to create new tariffs and to sell public lands. He vetoed

Tyler was against letting men vote if they did not own property.

John Tyler eventually had 15 children. He is shown here at a White House party celebrating his eldest grandchild's birthday.

bills until he felt Congress had improved them. But then Congress struck back. Tyler's secretary of the navy began a program to build steam-powered, iron ships. Congress introduced a bill to refuse payment for them. Of course, Tyler vetoed the bill. But then Congress used its power to overrule his veto, and the bill became law. This was the first time in history that Congress had successfully united to overturn a presidential veto.

Tyler proved to be better at taking over the presidency after Harrison's death than he was at actually being president. Despite his many battles with Congress, he was able to achieve some of his goals. The "log-cabin" bill allowed people to settle and improve public lands. Then they could purchase 160 acres for their families for a small fee, just $1.25 per acre. Tyler also helped settlers by recommending that trading posts be built. The Postal Reform Act of 1844 was one of Tyler's biggest successes. It lowered postal rates and added new services. It also recommended the use of the telegraph to send messages. The telegraph was a new invention that sent coded messages through electric wires. In the United States, the first practical telegraph system began in 1844, with a line between Baltimore, Maryland, and Washington, D.C.

Tyler had some success with foreign affairs, the nation's dealings with other countries. The Webster-Ashburton **Treaty** of 1842 was an agreement that settled the dispute over the boundary between Canada and Maine. Tyler also prevented the British from taking over Hawaii in 1842. He sent a group of advisors

Tyler's second wife, Julia, started the tradition of playing the song "Hail to the Chief" whenever a president appears at state events.

Samuel F. B. Morse (center) demonstrates his telegraph machine. Many people developed telegraph systems in the 1800s. Morse's became the one commonly used.

After James Polk became president in 1845, he used to say he was the "10th president elected by the people." Tyler was actually the 10th president, but Polk didn't believe he deserved the title because he hadn't been elected to the position.

to China in 1844. The result was the Treaty of Wang Hiya, which allowed U.S. ships to buy and sell goods in China.

In 1843, Tyler began secret talks with leaders in Texas, which was then an independent country. Many Texans wanted to become a part of the United States, and Tyler was in favor of this. He signed a treaty with the president of Texas, Sam Houston. But the U.S. Senate still had to approve it, and it refused to do so at first. Many senators did not want President Tyler to take credit for helping the nation grow. Also, the treaty said that slavery would be allowed in Texas, and many northern senators would not accept this.

As the election of 1844 drew near, neither the Democrats nor the Whigs wanted Tyler to be their

James Polk supported the expansion of the United States. Texas joined the Union during his presidency.

ANTI-TEXAS MEETING

AT FANEUIL HALL!

Friends of Freedom!

A proposition has been made, and will soon come up for consideration in the United States Senate, to annex Texas to the Union. This territory has been wrested from Mexico by violence and fraud. Such is the character of the leaders in this enterprise that the country has been aptly termed "that valley of rascals." It is large enough to make *nine* or *ten* States as large as Massachusetts. It was, under Mexico, a free territory. The freebooters have made it a slave territory. The design is to annex it, with its load of infamy and oppression, to the Union. The immediate result may be a war with Mexico—the ultimate result *will be* some 18 or 20 more slaveholders in the Senate of the United States, a still larger number in the House of Representatives, and the balance of power in the hands of the South! And if, when in a minority in Congress, slaveholders browbeat the North, demand the passage of gag laws, trample on the Right of Petition, and threaten, in defiance of the General Government, to hang every man, caught at the South, who dares to speak against their "domestic institutions," what limits shall be set to their intolerant demands and high handed usurpations, when they are in the majority?

All opposed to this scheme, of whatever sect or party, are invited to attend the meeting at the Old Cradle of Liberty, to-morrow, (Thursday Jan. 25,) at 10 o'clock, A. M., at which time addresses are expected from several able speakers.

Bostonians! Friends of Freedom!! Let your voices be heard in loud remonstrance against this scheme, fraught with such ruin to yourselves and such infamy to your country.

January 24, 1838.

presidential candidate. The Whigs chose Henry Clay, a highly regarded senator from Kentucky. The Democrats chose an unknown named James Polk. Most people had never even heard of Polk. But Polk was very much in favor of the **annexation** of Texas. He promised to help the nation expand across the continent.

Polk won the election. This showed Congress that Americans were in favor of having Texas join the nation. Three days before Tyler left office, Texas was admitted to the **Union.**

This poster advertised a meeting in Boston, Massachusetts, for people opposed to the annexation of Texas. John Tyler wanted Texas to join the Union, but many northerners opposed it because Texas would allow slavery.

THE NEW MRS. TYLER

Julia Gardiner was the daughter of a wealthy New York family. The beautiful young woman surprised her friends when she posed as a model for a department store advertisement. In the ad, she is shown carrying a small sign. "I'll purchase at Boger & Mecamly's," it reads. "Their goods are beautiful and astonishingly cheap."

Gardiner visited Washington, D.C., in 1842. She impressed everyone she met—including President Tyler. He had just lost his wife and felt lonely. Julia charmed him, and he asked her to marry him. She refused, but an accident changed her mind. Julia and her father, David Gardiner, were guests of the president on a new steamship, the *Princeton*. It was February 28, 1844. The captain of the ship wanted to show off the Peacemaker, the largest naval gun in the world. The third time it was fired, it exploded and killed David Gardiner and many others. President Tyler and Julia had been below deck and were unharmed. Tyler helped Julia get through the loss of her father. She grew to care greatly for him, and they married secretly four months later. They had seven children together. Tyler had a total of 15 children in his lifetime.

Julia Tyler served as first lady for the last eight months of her husband's term. She held several lively parties, including one for 3,000 guests. When the Tylers returned to live in Virginia, Julia helped run the family plantation. She also raised their many children.

After the Civil War, with her husband long dead, Julia had no money. She asked Congress for help. In 1870, she and Mary Lincoln, the widow of former president Abraham Lincoln, were given $1,200 each. After 1881, this amount was raised to $5,000 for all former first ladies. Julia lived her last eight years comfortably in Richmond and was buried at her husband's side.

GENTLEMAN FARMER

John and Julia Tyler were happy to return home to Virginia. Tyler said that when he was called to Washington after Harrison's death, "I foresaw that I was called to a bed of thorns. I now leave that bed which has afforded me little rest, and eagerly seek repose in the quiet enjoyments of rural life."

John Tyler in 1860

The Tylers' home was a 1,200-acre plantation called Sherwood Forest, which had been built in 1616. It was three miles (5 km) from Greenway, where Tyler had grown up. He had purchased it from his cousin in 1842 for $12,000. The Tylers named it Sherwood Forest in honor of the English outlaw Robin Hood, who lived in Sherwood Forest. Tyler saw himself as an outlaw, too, because he refused to do what the political parties expected of him. Tyler added a large ballroom to the

The dining room of Sherwood Forest, Tyler's home. Sherwood Forest is near Williamsburg, in southern Virginia.

mansion so people could dance the popular Virginia reel and enjoy parties at his home. This addition made it the longest wooden-frame house in America.

Tyler spent the next 17 years running his plantation. He enjoyed hunting foxes and other wild animals at Sherwood Forest. He played the violin for guests while Julia played the guitar. The family kept many pets and enjoyed their time together. Their life in Virginia was peaceful and pleasant.

Tyler did not leave public life completely after his presidency ended. In time, he rejoined the Democratic Party. In 1860, he became the chancellor of the College of William and Mary. This made him an important leader at the school.

William Henry Harrison once owned Tyler's Sherwood Forest home. It is the only house in the United States to be owned by two presidents.

In 1861, Tyler chaired the Peace Convention to try to work out a compromise between North and South.

Meanwhile, the nation was moving towards civil war. Abraham Lincoln was elected president in November 1860. Many southerners believed that he would end slavery. Some people argued that the southern states should **secede** from the Union. Lincoln argued that states could not leave the Union. He would fight to keep the Union whole.

Tyler returned to politics as chairman of the Peace Convention, a meeting that included people from 21 states. They all hoped to find a compromise that would prevent a war. When no solution could be found, Tyler recommended that Virginia leave the Union. In February 1861, South Carolina became the first state to secede. Ten more would soon follow. These states formed a new nation, the Confederate States of America. Its capital was first Montgomery, Alabama, and then Richmond, Virginia.

Jefferson Davis served as president of the Confederate States of America. He took the oath of office on the steps of the capitol in Montgomery, Alabama.

In November 1861, John Tyler was elected to the Confederate congress. The following January, Tyler went to Richmond to begin his work in the congress. Soon after he arrived, he was surprised to see his wife arrive at the hotel where he was staying. She had planned to join him there, but not for another week. Julia Tyler told her husband about a terrible nightmare she had had the night before. She dreamed that he was very ill and needed her help. She was so worried when she awoke that she decided to leave for Richmond at once. Tyler was pleased to see her, but he refused to worry about her dream. The next morning, though, he felt quite ill. Within two days, he was dead of bronchitis and a bad fever. His last words were, "Perhaps it is best." The Tyler family always believed that Julia's dream foresaw his death.

Many southern plantations were ruined during the Civil War. Sherwood Forest survived the war, but Union soldiers damaged the house and its furnishings. Today, visitors to the plantation can still see marks on the woodwork and doors from Civil War gunfire.

John Tyler died in 1862. He was 71 years old.

John and Julia Tyler had their seventh child when John was 70 years old.

Tyler, Texas, officially became a town in 1847. It is named for President John Tyler.

More than 150 carriages followed Tyler's coffin to Hollywood Cemetery in Richmond, Virginia. There Tyler was buried next to President James Monroe, the nation's fifth president.

Tyler was the only former president to join the Confederacy. For years after his death, many northerners considered him a traitor, someone who had betrayed his country. It was 53 years before the U.S. government put a memorial at his gravesite. Tyler probably would not have minded. Popularity was never important to him. Instead, he always stood up for his beliefs, even if they were unpopular.

THE GHOST OF SHERWOOD FOREST

The mansion at Sherwood Forest was old when John Tyler bought it in 1842. Tyler had to pay for its repair and he did much of the work on it himself. He even built "storm windows" for the house himself.

People said the mansion had been haunted for at least 50 years by the time he moved there with his family. And people say it has been haunted ever since. A ghost called the Gray Lady is said to roam the mansion.

Payne Tyler is married to John Tyler's grandson. She and her husband still live at Sherwood Forest. They are among the many Tyler family members and visitors who say they have seen the ghost. She says, "It is thought that she was a governess, who had charge of a small child at one time here. She would take the child from a first floor bedroom and walk her up through the hidden staircase to a second floor nursery. There, she would rock the child on her lap in a rocking chair. She is definitely in the house. I know, because I have personally had encounters with her."

1790	1800	1810	1820	1830

1790
John Tyler is born in Charles City County, Virginia, on March 29.

1802
Tyler begins classes at the College of William and Mary.

1807
Tyler graduates from the College of William and Mary. He begins to study law.

1809
Tyler passes his law exams. He moves to Richmond and works in the office of Edmund Randolph, who had been the nation's first attorney general.

1811
Tyler is elected to the Virginia House of Delegates. He holds this position until 1816.

1813
Tyler marries Letitia Christian on March 29, his 23rd birthday. They go on to have eight children.

1816
Tyler is elected to the U.S. House of Representatives. He holds the office from 1817 until 1821.

1823
Tyler becomes a member of the Virginia House of Delegates. He holds the position until 1825.

1825
Tyler is elected governor of Virginia. He holds the position for two terms.

1827
Tyler enters the U.S. Senate. He remains in office for nine years.

1828
Tyler supports Andrew Jackson in the presidential election because they have similar views on the Second Bank of the United States and states' rights. Jackson is elected president.

1833
Tyler opposes Jackson's Force Bill, which gives the president the power to send federal troops into a state that refuses to obey presidential orders.

1834
Tyler and other senators censure Jackson after he removed government funds from the Second Bank of the United States.

1836

The state of Virginia orders Tyler to cancel his censure of President Jackson. Tyler refuses and resigns his seat in the Senate. He quits the Democratic Party and joins the Whigs, a political party formed to oppose Jackson.

1838

Tyler returns to the Virginia legislature for two years.

1839

Tyler is elected Speaker of the Virginia House of Delegates.

1840

The Whigs nominate William Henry Harrison as their presidential candidate and Tyler as their vice presidential candidate. Harrison and Tyler win the election.

1841

Tyler is vice president for only one month before William Henry Harrison dies on April 4. Tyler takes the oath of office on April 9. All but one of Harrison's Whig cabinet members quit their jobs.

1842

The Webster-Ashburton Treaty settles a boundary dispute between Maine and Canada. Tyler promises to protect Hawaii from invasion by foreign powers. Letitia Christian Tyler dies on September 10 at age 51. She is the first wife of a president to die while her husband is in office.

1843

Tyler begins secret meetings with Sam Houston, the president of Texas, hoping to finalize the annexation of Texas. They come to an agreement and sign a treaty. The Senate refuses to approve the treaty.

1844

The treaty of Wang Hiya gives the United States access to Chinese ports. Tyler marries Julia Gardiner in June. Recognizing he has little chance to win the election, Tyler does not run for president. James K. Polk, who strongly favors the annexation of Texas, wins the election.

1845

Congress agrees to the annexation of Texas. Tyler signs an act admitting it to the Union three days before he leaves office. He and Julia return to Virginia to live at their plantation, Sherwood Forest.

1860

Tyler is named chancellor of the College of William and Mary.

1861

Tyler serves as chairman of the Peace Convention in Washington, D.C. Members of the convention try to reach a compromise to avoid a civil war. They are unable to reach an agreement, and war breaks out on April 12. Tyler is elected to the Congress of the Confederate States of America.

1862

Tyler dies in Richmond, Virginia, on January 18.

GLOSSARY

annexation (an-ek-SAY-shun) Annexation is the joining of something smaller (such as a territory) to something bigger (such as a country). Tyler was in favor of the annexation of Texas to the United States.

bill (BIL) A bill is an idea for a new law that is presented to a group of lawmakers. Tyler vetoed many bills that were introduced by Congress.

cabinet (KAB-nit) A cabinet is the group of people who advise a president. All but one member of Harrison's cabinet resigned shortly after Tyler took office.

campaign (kam-PAYN) A campaign is the process of running for an election, including activities such as giving speeches or attending rallies. During their campaign, Jackson and Van Buren promised more opportunities to common people.

candidate (KAN-duh-dayt) A candidate is a person running in an election. The Whigs chose Tyler as their vice presidential candidate in 1840.

compromise (KOM-pruh-myz) A compromise is a way to settle a disagreement in which both sides give up part of what they want. Tyler would not support the Missouri Compromise.

constitution (kon-stih-TOO-shun) A constitution is the set of basic principles that govern a state, country, or society. Tyler believed in the principles of the U.S. Constitution.

federal (FED-ur-ul) Federal refers to the national government of the United States, rather than a state or city government. Tyler believed the states should have more power than the federal government.

frontier (frun-TEER) A frontier is a region that is at the edge of or beyond settled land. The U.S. government gave public land to homesteaders on the frontier.

gentry (JEN-tree) The gentry is the ruling class. Tyler was a member of the Virginia gentry.

impeachment (im-PEECH-munt) Impeachment is when the House of Representatives charges a president with a crime or serious misdeed. Some congressmen thought President Tyler should face impeachment.

inauguration (ih-naw-gyuh-RAY-shun) An inauguration is the ceremony that takes place when a new president begins a term. William Henry Harrison's inauguration took place on a cold and rainy day.

legislature (LEJ-uh-slay-chur) A legislature is the part of a government that makes laws. Tyler was elected to the Virginia state legislature.

pneumonia (nuh-MOHN-yuh) Pneumonia is a disease of the lungs. President Harrison died from pneumonia.

political party (puh-LIT-uh-kul PAR-tee) A political party is a group of people who share similar ideas about how to run a government. Tyler joined the Democratic political party in 1827.

politics (PAWL-uh-tiks) Politics refers to the actions and practices of the government. Tyler began his long career in politics with the Virginia state legislature.

principles (PRIN-suh-puls) Principles are basic beliefs, or what people believe to be right and true. Tyler firmly believed in the principles of the Constitution.

secede (suh-SEED) If a group secedes, it separates from a larger group. South Carolina was the first southern state to secede from the Union.

statesmen (STAYTZ-men) Statesmen are people skilled at managing public or national affairs. Tyler said he was glad to have able statesmen in his cabinet.

tariff (TAYR-iff) A tariff is a tax on goods brought in from other countries. Tyler vetoed a tariff bill in 1842.

territories (TAIR-uh-tor-eez) Territories are lands or regions, especially lands that belong to a government. The U.S. government had to decide whether to allow slavery in its new territories.

treaty (TREE-tee) A treaty is a formal agreement between nations. Tyler signed a treaty with the president of Texas in 1843.

unconstitutional (un-kon-stih-TOO-shuh-nel) Unconstitutional means going against the Constitution of the United States. Tyler opposed any law that he believed was unconstitutional.

union (YOON-yen) A union is the joining together of two people or groups of people, such as states. The Union is another name for the United States.

vetoed (VEE-tohd) A president vetoed a bill if he refused to sign it. Tyler vetoed two bills establishing a national bank.

THE UNITED STATES GOVERNMENT

The United States government is divided into three equal branches: the executive, the legislative, and the judicial. This division helps prevent abuses of power because each branch has to answer to the other two. No one branch can become too powerful.

EXECUTIVE BRANCH

PRESIDENT
VICE PRESIDENT
DEPARTMENTS

The job of the executive branch is to enforce the laws. It is headed by the president, who serves as the spokesperson for the United States around the world. The president signs bills into law and appoints important officials such as federal judges. He or she is also the commander in chief of the U.S. military. The president is assisted by the vice president, who takes over if the president dies or cannot carry out the duties of the office.

The executive branch also includes various departments, each focused on a specific topic. They include the Defense Department, the Justice Department, and the Agriculture Department. The department heads, along with other officials such as the vice president, serve as the president's closest advisers, called the cabinet.

LEGISLATIVE BRANCH

CONGRESS
Senate and
House of Representatives

The job of the legislative branch is to make the laws. It consists of Congress, which is divided into two parts: the Senate and the House of Representatives. The Senate has 100 members, and the House of Representatives has 435 members. Each state has two senators. The number of representatives a state has varies depending on the state's population.

Besides making laws, Congress also passes budgets and enacts taxes. In addition, it is responsible for declaring war, maintaining the military, and regulating trade with other countries.

JUDICIAL BRANCH

SUPREME COURT
COURTS OF APPEALS
DISTRICT COURTS

The job of the judicial branch is to interpret the laws. It consists of the nation's federal courts. Trials are held in district courts. During trials, judges must decide what laws mean and how they apply. Courts of appeals review the decisions made in district courts.

The nation's highest court is the Supreme Court. If someone disagrees with a court of appeals ruling, he or she can ask the Supreme Court to review it. The Supreme Court may refuse. The Supreme Court makes sure that decisions and laws do not violate the Constitution.

CHOOSING
THE PRESIDENT

It may seem odd, but American voters don't elect the president directly. Instead, the president is chosen using what is called the Electoral College.

Each state gets as many votes in the Electoral College as its combined total of senators and representatives in Congress. For example, Iowa has two senators and five representatives, so it gets seven electoral votes. Although the District of Columbia does not have any voting members in Congress, it gets three electoral votes. Usually, the candidate who wins the most votes in any given state receives all of that state's electoral votes.

To become president, a candidate must get more than half of the Electoral College votes. There are a total of 538 votes in the Electoral College, so a candidate needs 270 votes to win. If nobody receives 270 Electoral College votes, the House of Representatives chooses the president.

With the Electoral College system, the person who receives the most votes nationwide does not always receive the most electoral votes. This happened most recently in 2000, when Al Gore received half a million more national votes than George W. Bush. Bush became president because he had more Electoral College votes.

THE WHITE HOUSE

The White House is the official home of the president of the United States. It is located at 1600 Pennsylvania Avenue NW in Washington, D.C. In 1792, a contest was held to select the architect who would design the president's home. James Hoban won. Construction took eight years.

The first president, George Washington, never lived in the White House. The second president, John Adams, moved into the house in 1800, though the inside was not yet complete. During the War of 1812, British soldiers burned down much of the White House. It was rebuilt several years later.

The White House was changed through the years. Porches were added, and President Theodore Roosevelt added the West Wing. President William Taft changed the shape of the presidential office, making it into the famous Oval Office. While Harry Truman was president, the old house was discovered to be structurally weak. All the walls were reinforced with steel, and the rooms were rebuilt.

Today, the White House has 132 rooms (including 35 bathrooms), 28 fireplaces, and 3 elevators. It takes 570 gallons of paint to cover the outside of the six-story building. The White House provides the president with many ways to relax. It includes a putting green, a jogging track, a swimming pool, a tennis court, and beautifully landscaped gardens. The White House also has a movie theater, a billiard room, and a one-lane bowling alley.

PRESIDENTIAL PERKS

The job of president of the United States is challenging. It is probably one of the most stressful jobs in the world. Because of this, presidents are paid well, though not nearly as well as the leaders of large corporations. In 2007, the president earned $400,000 a year. Presidents also receive extra benefits that make the demanding job a little more appealing.

★ **Camp David:** In the 1940s, President Franklin D. Roosevelt chose this heavily wooded spot in the mountains of Maryland to be the presidential retreat, where presidents can relax. Even though it is a retreat, world business is conducted there. Most famously, President Jimmy Carter met with Middle Eastern leaders at Camp David in 1978. The result was a peace agreement between Israel and Egypt.

★ *Air Force One:* The president flies on a jet called *Air Force One*. It is a Boeing 747-200B that has been modified to meet the president's needs.

Air Force One is the size of a large home. It is equipped with a dining room, sleeping quarters, a conference room, and office space. It also has two kitchens that can provide food for up to 50 people.

★ **The Secret Service:** While not the most glamorous of the president's perks, the Secret Service is one of the most important. The Secret Service is a group of highly trained agents who protect the president and the president's family.

★ **The Presidential State Car:** The presidential limousine is a stretch Cadillac DTS.

It has been armored to protect the president in case of attack. Inside the plush car are a foldaway desk, an entertainment center, and a communications console.

★ **The Food:** The White House has five chefs who will make any food the president wants. The White House also has an extensive wine collection.

★ **Retirement:** A former president receives a pension, or retirement pay, of just under $180,000 a year. Former presidents also receive Secret Service protection for the rest of their lives.

F A C T S

QUALIFICATIONS

To run for president, a candidate must

* ★ be at least 35 years old
* ★ be a citizen who was born in the United States
* ★ have lived in the United States for 14 years

TERM OF OFFICE

A president's term of office is four years.
No president can stay in office for more than two terms.

ELECTION DATE

The presidential election takes place every four years on the first Tuesday of November.

INAUGURATION DATE

Presidents are inaugurated on January 20.

OATH OF OFFICE

I do solemnly swear I will faithfully execute the office of the President of the United States and will to the best of my ability preserve, protect, and defend the Constitution of the United States.

WRITE A LETTER TO THE PRESIDENT

One of the best things about being a U.S. citizen is that Americans get to participate in their government. They can speak out if they feel government leaders aren't doing their jobs. They can also praise leaders who are going the extra mile. Do you have something you'd like the president to do? Should the president worry more about the environment and encourage people to recycle? Should the government spend more money on our schools? You can write a letter to the president to say how you feel!

1600 Pennsylvania Avenue
Washington, D.C. 20500
You can even send an e-mail to: president@whitehouse.gov

BOOKS

Barber, James. *Presidents.* New York: Dorling Kindersley Publishers, 2000.

Bausm, Ann. *Our Country's Presidents.* Washington, DC: National Geographic Society, 2005.

DeMauro, Lisa, and the editors of *TIME for Kids. Presidents of the United States.* New York: Harper Collins Publishers, 2006.

Doak, Robin S. *John Tyler.* Minneapolis, MN: Compass Point Books, 2003.

Feinberg, Barbara Silberdick. *America's First Ladies.* New York: Franklin Watts, 1998.

Morris, Juddi. *At Home With the Presidents.* New York: John Wiley & Sons, 1999.

Ochester, Betsy. *John Tyler: America's 10th President.* New York: Children's Press, 2003.

VIDEOS

The History Channel Presents The Presidents. DVD (New York: A&E Home Video, 2005).

National Geographic's Inside the White House. DVD (Washington, DC: National Geographic Video, 2003).

INTERNET SITES

Visit our Web page for lots of links about John Tyler and other U.S. presidents:

http://www.childsworld.com/links

Note to Parents, Teachers, and Librarians: We routinely verify our Web links to make sure they are safe, active sites—so encourage your readers to check them out!

INDEX